P9-CFF-141

Palmistry
by Lauren David Peden

THE MYSTICAL ARTS

Illustrations by Jenny Tylden Wright

WARNER ⊕ TREASURES
PUBLISHED BY WARNER BOOKS
A TIME WARNER COMPANY

Copyright © 1996 by Lauren David Peden

All rights reserved.

Book design by Diane Luger

Illustrations by Jenny Tylden Wright

Warner Treasures is a
trademark of Warner Books, Inc.

Warner Books, Inc.,
1271 Avenue of the Americas,
New York, NY 10020

 A Time Warner Company

Printed in China
First Printing: March 1996

10 9 8 7 6 5 4 3 2 1

ISBN: 0-446-91014-7

Palmistry

THE MYSTICAL ARTS

In the art of palmistry, our personalities, aptitudes, and potentials are all reflected in our hands. A study of the hand reveals the state of a person's physical health, emotional nature, prospects for success in love and business, creative capacities, individuality, and spirituality. Hand shape, finger length, skin texture, mounts and lines all form a sort of topographical map of the psyche. Through this map, we can gain valuable insight into our talents, inclinations, and limitations.

Hand analysis can provide us with an opportunity to learn more about our inner selves and to use that knowledge to find fulfillment in all areas of life. The hand mirrors our life experience—past, present, and future—and palmistry provides a wonderful opportunity to help us chart our progress and realize our potential.

HOW TO READ A PALM

Palmists divide the hands into two categories: major and minor. The major hand is the one you use most often; the other hand is the minor hand. A hand analysis should begin with a brief examination of the minor (subjective) hand, which represents the intrinsic qualities you are born with—inclinations and innate capabilities. The reading continues with an in-depth examination of the major (objective) hand, which shows how you have developed those qualities and what you've made of your life so far.

First, have the person rest the hands, palms-down, on the tabletop so you can observe the shape of the hands and nails, and the spread of the fingers. Then turn the hand over so you can evaluate the color and temperature of the palm and see the clarity of the lines. Also check out the shape and length of the fingers, as well as the knottiness or smoothness of the knuckles. Test both hands for flexibility—at the wrist, finger joints, and thumb, and look at the spread of the thumb in relation to the hand. Push on the center of the palm to evaluate its elasticity, and test the ball of the thumb and the mounts for firmness and fullness. Finish up by examining the primary, secondary, and minor lines, and any major markings, such as the angle of luck, the Battle Cross, stars, squares, triangles, and so forth.

Before you start to read the mounts and lines, gently caress the middle of the palm with your thumb. There's an artery located under the ball of the thumb, and some people believe that there's also a psychic center in the palm of the hand that, when stimulated, will help you to communicate the things of importance you see during a palm reading.

When it comes to relaying bad news, proceed with caution. If you see signs of potential illness or a stroke of bad luck reflected in the hand, temper the information. If, for instance, you see love trouble ahead, you could say something like, "For the most part, your marriage looks pretty solid, but there may be some minor conflicts on the horizon. You might want to focus more attention on your relationship in the next few months." If you run into a hand that's confusing or hard to decipher, ask the person for specific questions to be answered. As a beginner, it's best to focus on the main areas of interest (love, money, success, travel). If you have trouble identifying the lines, try outlining them with a soft lead pencil or washable ink pen. The best hand to read first is, of course, your own, followed by the hands of family members and friends. This enables you to compare what you see in the hand with what you already know to be true.

HAND SHAPES

The shape of a person's hand can tell you a lot about their character, personality, and disposition. The five fundamental shapes are square, pointed, conical, spatulate, and mixed (the last accounts for most modern hand types; few people have a pure hand shape).

THE SQUARE HAND: The fingers on a square hand appear blunt—as if they were chopped off—and may be long or short in length. The skin is usually firm and smooth and the fingers somewhat inflexible. The lower mounts (moon and Venus) are well developed, while the upper mounts run together in a single ridge. The lines are usually deep and clear, indicating an intense personality. They tend to be short, and except for the life line, run straight—the mark of a realist. People with square hands (especially those with long fingers) are very successful in the world of business and have no problem making money. They have solid, traditional values and are scrupulously honest in their dealings with others. They are trustworthy, devoted romantic partners. Square-handed people often have strong spiritual beliefs. They're generally very healthy and tremendously energetic.

THE POINTED HAND: Pointed hands have thin, tapering fingers and appear delicate and graceful. The thumb is often long and flexible. The skin tends to be almost translucent, and the lines are often very fine. The fate line is usually distinct, and the heart and head lines may curve up toward the ring finger, indicating an artistic bent. The knuckles are usually smooth, denoting a rather dreamy nature (knotty joints give this hand more practical leanings). People with pointed hands are usually introverted, idealistic, and highly intuitive—even psychic. They enjoy caring for others, and make excellent therapists, teachers or nurses. They love the arts and appreciate aesthetic beauty. In relationships, people with pointed hands like to be taken care of. Spiritual relationships take precedence over physical needs. They generally have delicate constitutions, and are susceptible to colds, lung conditions, and nervous disorders.

THE CONICAL HAND: This hand combines long, tubular fingers and a full, fleshy palm. It is somewhat tapered, but appears rounder than the other types of hands. The skin is usually fine-textured. The lines may be wavery, and the head and heart lines often point down toward the Mount of the Moon, indicating a creative and imaginative nature. If the fingers are knotty, this denotes a philosophical, original thinker. People with conical hands excel in artistic careers. They have friendly, gentle natures and are capable of great affection. They have an overwhelming need to be admired by others, and their desire for romance and love overrides their desire for sex. Their health is somewhat fragile. They tend to be impulsive and superstitious, and need to guard against neurosis.

THE SPATULATE HAND: This type of hand is narrow at the base and fans out into a wide palm (or vice versa), and is coupled with broad, thick fingertips. The fingers are often knotty, and the thumb is usually long, suggesting an ambitious, can-do attitude. The skin texture tends to be average. The lines are usually strong, clear and plentiful, signifying a lot of activity. People with spatulate hands have quizzical, inquiring minds and extroverted personalities. They are great communicators, and are quick to share their enthusiasm with others. These are the active, hands-on hands found on scientists, journalists, sculptors, therapists, and entrepreneurs. They love to share activities with their partners. They're intellectually curious and are always searching for the "real truth" (especially when it comes to spirituality). Physically, people with spatulate hands love to eat and are exceptionally healthy.

THE MIXED HAND: This is the most common hand shape, and it combines the elements of all the other hand types—square, conical, pointed, and spatulate—in both the fingers and the palm. To evaluate this hand accurately, look for the one shape that dominates the others; if a hand is 70 percent square and 30 percent conical, the square shape predominates, and you should base your reading accordingly. On the other hand (so to speak), a person with a spatulate palm and knotty, conical fingers could be defined as a creative type with an ambitious nature who needs to overcome shyness in order to realize their goals. A truly mixed hand has different finger shapes and a palm that is somewhat oblong, with a rounded heel and square thumb base. This hand marks a versatile person, and it belongs to someone who is as practical as they are creative. To fully understand any hand, however, you need to examine the mounts and lines, as well.

FLEXIBILITY: Generally speaking, the more flexible the hand, the more flexible the person. A hand that easily bends backward at the wrist indicates an open-minded, easygoing nature. But if the fingers bend back really far, the person may be too easily swayed by the opinions and attitudes of others. Stiff hands and fingers typically indicate a rigid personality—except in the case of a stiff thumb, which is the sign of a strong will. If the fingers are cramped and curl inward like claws, the person is afraid of life's challenges and tends to get stuck in a routine. Ever notice how pliable children's hands are? That's because they're still open to new experiences.

The elasticity of the palm can also reveal a lot about a person's attitude toward life. People with hard, inflexible palms don't respond to life, perhaps out of fear; they let new experiences bounce off them and don't absorb much. People with overly soft palms have no spring to their nature and don't easily bounce back from failure. They tend to stifle their emotions and don't enjoy taking risks. Normal, elastic palms are the sign of a resilient, tolerant attitude. These people tend to have a positive outlook and an easy sense of give and take.

COLOR: To determine hand color, look at the person's palms. A pale palm is a sign of physical exhaustion and emotional hopelessness. A pink palm denotes a cheerful, optimistic attitude, good circulation, and a healthy aggressiveness. People with red palms are often pushy and hyperactive, and may be given to temper tantrums. A yellow palm indicates a lack of vitality and a jaundiced, inhibited nature (which may be psychologically induced or caused by a malfunctioning liver).

TEXTURE: Skin texture can give us clues to a person's general outlook. People with fine, smooth skin usually have refined tastes and appreciate aesthetic beauty and creature comforts. Rough skin indicates people who will do whatever it takes to achieve their goals, but who have a tendency to trample on others along the way. Average skin texture happily marries an efficient, practical nature with a sense of empathy toward others.

TEMPERATURE: People with warm hands are generally in good health and have a balanced, healthy outlook on life. People with hot hands are bursting with physical energy. They're usually intense, and they approach every situation with great passion. Cold hands indicate an anxious, overly sensitive nature. These people may be afraid to throw themselves into life, and may hold back as a result.

THE THUMB AND FINGERS
Once the general shape of the hand is identi-

fied, it's time to consider the thumb and fingers. To palmists, the thumbs are the most significant digits. The thumb holds a peculiar position through its complete independence from the other four fingers and its wide range of mobility. It symbolizes the advancement of our species—our individuality and our ability to speak, think, and feel—the very qualities that distinguish us from animals. It is for this reason that we look first to the thumb when reading someone's hand.

The thumb can be seen as the base on which the whole hand rests, and any irregularity in this digit is of greater significance than an irregularity in any other aspect of the hand (people with mental disabilities, for instance, tend to have shorter thumbs than the general population). When the hand is spread, the thumb should stand at a reasonable distance from the palm (if the index finger points north, the thumb should point northwest). The wider the angle between the thumb and forefinger, the more generous and compassionate the nature. If the thumb clings to the side of the hand for dear life and is unyielding to pressure, it's indicative of a cautious, possibly fearful mind-set. It should be possible to bend the top joint slightly backward; the farther back the thumb joint bends, the more flexible and easygoing its owner is thought to be. Conversely, a stiff, unyielding thumb indicates a strong will and a somewhat rigid nature.

Next, look at the overall shape of the thumbs. A well-formed thumb is slightly waisted (tapered in the middle), indicating a balanced, diplomatic nature. Thick thumbs indicate a stubborn streak, extremely thick thumbs may suggest violent tendencies, and a very slender thumb connotes patience.

Although considered less important than the thumb, the size and shape of the fingers are also significant. The fingers represent a person's conscious energy and awareness and their ability to communicate with the outside world, both figuratively and literally, through the sense of touch. The fingers tell us how we utilize the various qualities stored within our being, each of which is represented by a different digit. The index finger is associated with authority, ambition, self-assertiveness, and public image. The middle finger concerns stability, vocation, duty, and reason; it separates the active and passive sides of the hand and also serves to unite them. The ring finger pertains to aesthetic fulfillment, service to others, and the emotions, and the little finger has to do with one's behavior and interaction with the outside world.

Long, slim fingers suggest that the intellect rules the emotions; short, thick fingers suggest that the physical nature dominates mental reasoning. Normally, the middle finger is the longest, followed by the index, ring, and pinky fingers. Any deviation from the norm has psychological implications and places greater emphasis on the specific characteristics of the predominant finger. Look at the palm side of the hand to assess the length and shape of the fingers. An average-length index finger (one that reaches the center of the middle finger's top joint) suggests a reliable person with a healthy dose of ambition; a long index finger indicates an

Pointed
Conic
Spade Shape
Square

authoritative nature; an extremely long index finger suggests an arrogant, quarrelsome person; and a short index finger represents uncertainty and a lack of self-confidence.

An average-length middle finger (it should be the same size as the width of the hand at the base of the fingers) suggests the ability to concentrate and get the job done; a long middle finger (one that's as long as the palm itself) suggests a discerning but cautious nature; an extremely long middle finger highlights a tendency toward introversion, pessimism, and loneliness; and a short middle finger means that the person is intuitive rather than intellectual.

An average-length ring finger (one that is almost as long as the index finger) indicates emotional stability and a warm magnanimous personality;

a long ring finger indicates artistic tendencies and an excess of egotism; an extremely long ring finger suggests a fickle, irresponsible, attention-grabbing nature; and a short ring finger is indicative of an introverted, withdrawn nature.

An average-length pinky (one that reaches the top crease of the ring finger) symbolizes a fanciful and impetuous outlook; a long pinky suggests a perceptive, clever nature and a heightened sense of expression; an extremely long pinky denotes a devious, untrustworthy person who's overly concerned with material gains; and a short pinky indicates a person who is uncommitted and has trouble reaching their potential.

The finger shapes are also relevant in assessing a person's character. Conical fingers stress the imaginative-intuitive approach of a sensitive person, and show a willingness to consider the opinions of others. Pointed, tapered fingers indicate a shy, kind person with great reserves of patience and artistic sensibilities. They also indicate a lack of initiative and willpower. Square fingers suggest a realistic, down-to-earth person who bases judgments on solid facts. Spatulate fingers have the same qualities as square fingers, coupled with inventiveness, a magnanimous nature, and tons of physical energy. These people know what they want and they go after it with a vengeance. Of course, many people have mixed finger shapes, which indicates great diversity and varied talents. These people enjoy a broad range of interests.

The fingernails can also give an indication of a person's physical, mental, and emotional well-being. To determine a nail's shape, look at its width and the shape of its base, not at the shape of the manicured tip. Broad nails indicate good physical health and a broad outlook on life. These people tend to be cheerful and extroverted, and are open to new experiences and different points of view. Very broad and flat nails, however, indicate an obstinate, somewhat defensive personality. Square nails denote practicality and a healthy curiosity about people and life in general. This nail shape suggests a well-balanced personality. Oval nails are indicative of an idealistic, quick-witted, and sociable nature. Long, pointed nails suggest a delicate, somewhat frail constitution and a hasty, indiscriminate intellect. These people appreciate harmony and aesthetic beauty. Short nails connote average health and a critical, analytical mindset. People with very short nails are usually quick-tempered. Spatulate nails are the sign of a nervous perfectionist who is overly concerned with the opinions of others. Vertical ridges on the nails suggest that the

Apollo

Saturn

jupiter

Mars Negative *

ury

Mercury

sitive

Positive

(Luna)

Venus

person is high-strung and prone to agitation. Horizontal ridges indicate a recent trauma.

In general, the flexibility of the fingers indicates the flexibility of our character. If the fingers can be pushed far back from the wrist, we have a supple, give-and-take nature. Likewise, if the top phalanx of the finger flexes easily, the person tends to be easygoing. A stiff, inflexible nail phalanx suggests an unyielding person with strong defense mechanisms. If the top joint bends back too far, however, the person may be too accepting or even self-destructively uninhibited.

THE MOUNTS

If hand shapes represent our basic character and the thumb symbolizes our motivation, then the eight mounts represent our general behavior. They are thought to reflect the traits, personality quirks, and special interests that make each of us unique. The mounts appear as raised pads of flesh on the palm under the four fingers, at the base of the thumb, on the heel of the hand, and at the inner and outer sides of the hand. They're named for the moon and planets, and the connection between the traits of each mount and the character of its corresponding heavenly body will be apparent to anyone familiar with astrology. Generally, the mounts are slightly raised and visible, but not terribly pronounced. A well-developed mount indicates that the traits associated with it are strong, an underdeveloped or flat mount means the traits are dormant, and an overdeveloped mount suggests excess.

The Mount of Jupiter lies directly below the index finger and, like the forefinger itself, is associated with ambition and social interaction. A flat mount indicates a healthy sense of motivation and a sound balance between work and pleasure. If it's flat, it suggests laziness, procrastination, and low self-esteem. A prominent mount indicates over aggressiveness, an insatiable need for public recognition, and a thoughtless disregard for others. If the pad drifts toward the middle finger, it suggests a more conservative, practical way of approaching life. If the heart line arises on this mount, and is accompanied by a strong marriage line, it indicates a loving, fulfilling union.

The Mount of Saturn lies below the middle finger and is associated with sobriety and reason. In most hands, this mount is not developed, which is the preferred characteristic.

If it's noticeable and firm, this mount indicates a very serious, almost disagreeable disposition (causing the person to feel alienated and lonely, as well). A large, soft mount denotes a tendency toward morbid thinking. If it's very pronounced, it suggests extreme introversion and possible paranoia.

The Mount of Apollo lies below the ring finger and is connected with an individual's artistic nature. A normal-sized mount indicates a comfortable grasp of aesthetics and a natural inclination to shine; these people radiate warmth, and others are instinctively drawn to them. A mount that is prominent or overly soft suggests a tendency toward self-indulgence, boastfulness, and pie-in-the-sky daydreams. A flat mount connotes a dull, unperceptive nature and lack of enthusiasm. If this mount drifts toward the middle finger, the artistic tendencies are tempered with philosophical realism. If it drifts toward the pinky, it indicates one who prefers the business side of aesthetic pursuits.

The Mount of Mercury lies beneath the little finger and has to do with memory, communication skills, and how we actual-ize our overall potential. If the mount is well developed, this denotes an agile wit, business acumen, and financial savvy. If it's very prominent, it signifies a devious, double-dealing character. If it's very flat, it suggests impracticality, naiveté, and limited verbal ability.

The Mount of Venus lies just below the thumb (in fact, it functions as the thumb's third phalanx); it represents passion. A well-developed mount indicates that the person really enjoys life, and is able to give and receive love—physical, emotional, and spiri-tual—freely. A high mount of Venus can sig-nify an overwhelming emotional or sexual neediness, and an underdeveloped mount implies that the person has a low sex drive and no zest for life.

The Lower Mount of Mars (Negative) lies on the inside of the palm just above the Mount of Venus, and it represents physical courage. A normal-sized mount suggests general enthusiasm coupled with the ability to persevere. A prominent mount indicates fearlessness and arrogance, while a flat mount points to hesitancy—even cowardice—and a lack of assertiveness.

The Upper Mount of Mars (Positive) lies on the outside of the palm just above the Mount of the Moon, and is associated with moral fiber and mental strength. A well-developed mount indicates a pragmatic, well-balanced character. An overdeveloped mount reveals a dominant streak and a potential for cruelty. An underdeveloped mount indicates a weak resolve and apathetic nature. If the head line runs into this mount, the person has a great deal of common sense.

The Mount of the Moon, or Luna, is located on the heel of the hand, opposite the Mount of Venus. It is connected with intuition and creativity. A normal mount indicates a healthy imagination. A conspicuous mount suggests difficulty separating fantasy from reality, and a flat mount is the mark of an uninspired thinker.

THE PRIMARY LINES

With few exceptions, the palm contains three major, or primary, lines: The life line, the head line, and the heart line. These lines are linked with the qualities of will, wisdom, and love, respectively. Because these lines are more deeply rooted in our subconscious than are the other lines in the palm, they change less quickly. We evaluate the lines according to their position, length, solidity, and curvature. It's important to observe precisely where a line begins and ends. The beginning of the line indicates the intention, the course of the line shows the direction of the energy, and the end of the line signifies the ultimate purpose. In general, if a line is unbroken, it is considered sound (breaks in a line indicate changes, often problematic). A frayed or feathered line is a sign of frailty. A faint, shallow line denotes superficiality and a lack of energy; an unusually deep line signifies extreme intensity. The lines are the energy links between the mounts; they symbolize the interaction between the various parts of our character. A line that forks at the end refers to the mount at which it points. A double (or "sister") line intensifies the meaning of the line be-side it, and it is a sign of protective good fortune. To determine when specific events occurred (or are likely to occur) in a person's lifetime, divide the line into thirds (each of which represents a

twenty-five- to thirty-year period). The first third is youth; the middle third, adulthood; and the last third, old age. This will help you give a more accurate reading.

The Life Line represents our physical condition and the nature of our life force. Contrary to popular belief, the length of the line does not predict the length of one's life, but rather, indicates a person's level of vitality. Although this line primarily reflects the physical aspects of our life, it also gives us clues to our psychological and spiritual makeup. It shows, for instance, whether we approach life with timidity or gusto. The longer the line, the greater the energy resources (although a short line, if deep, is also auspicious). The Life Line normally begins on the inside of the palm between the thumb and index finger, and curves down to the base of the thumb. A strong downward curve indicates strength; a relatively straight line suggests limited stamina; a wide arc is indicative of an outgoing nature, while a narrow arc suggests shyness; and an unusually wide arc indicates a huge, almost insatiable, appetite for life. A line that curves around to the Mount of Venus indicates strength, enthusiasm, and a happy, harmonious home life. A line that runs close to the thumb indicates a lack of physical energy and an overly cautious temperament. A line that runs down to the heel of the hand toward the Mount of the Moon suggests an imaginative nature and a peripatetic lifestyle.

If the line is thin or wavery, or if there are smaller lines branching off the Life Line, it suggests uneven health. A chained line is indicative of a worrisome, emotional nature (small lines crossing the Life Line also indicate worries). A cross on the line signifies danger, while a square denotes protective forces at work. An island in the Life Line indicates illness or exhaustion; a star represents a serious crisis. A line that forks at the end may suggest a warring need for both security and adventure. A broken line indicates a lack of direction or a past illness; if the line continues elsewhere in the hand, it indicates that the quality of life was restored. Small lines branching up from the Life Line connote an ability to recover from setbacks; downward-pointing lines indicate wasted energy. A double (sister) line indicates an especially vital nature.

The Head Line represents our intellectual capabilities and our ability to relate to the outside world. The Head Line normally begins on the inside of the palm, just under the Mount of Jupiter, and runs straight across the hand. If there is only one line running across the palm, it is the Head Line. If there are two lines running almost parallel to each other, the Head Line is the lower of the two. Ideally, the lines should stand apart on the hand, indicating a separation between the qualities of will, wisdom and love. If the head and life line merge at their origin (which is not all that uncommon), this indicates that the intellect is influenced by physical consciousness. People with this line tend to worry too much about how others perceive them. Lines that are separate connote a love of adventure and an enthusiastic outlook. The farther the Head Line is from the Life Line, the more independent the thought process. If the line arises in the Mount of Jupiter, the person's intellect is tempered by idealism and ambition. The longer the line, the more abstract the thinking and greater the ability to focus; a long Head Line also indicates a retentive memory. A short line denotes the ability to accumulate material possessions in a practical manner (a short, deep line indicates that the person's interests are narrow but intense). The depth of this line reflects the degree of analytical capability. A deep line suggests a love of acquiring knowledge, reading books, and the like. A thin, wavery line indicates a lack of concentration, though not necessarily a lack of intellect. Besides representing mental and intellectual prowess, the Head Line also has a lot to do with our attitudes toward life, philosophy, and the way we handle problems. A strong downward curve (toward the Mount of the Moon) denotes an imaginative and creative mind. If the line ends between the Mounts of the Moon and Upper Mars, it indicates a happy balance between imaginative and analytical thinking. A relatively straight line is the mark of a practical thinker. A short Head Line that curves upward at the end is the sign of a scatterbrain.

Tiny lines branching off the Head Line indicate distractions that hamper intellectual productivity. Little lines that dissect the Head Line represent life-changing decisions. A fork at the end indicates a choice between two forms of thinking (linear or creative), or a tendency toward indecisiveness. An island in the Head Line indicates blocked energy and suggests mental confusion or an intellectual dilemma of some sort. A chained line indicates tension; a cross denotes a mental crisis. A star on the line represents an outstanding mental achievement, while a square shows guidance. If the head and heart lines are widely separated, it's an indication of early independence.

The Heart Line represents our emotional capabilities as well as the physical condition of the heart itself. The whole spectrum of feelings—from a lack of self-love to sexuality to overall attitudes toward love— can be read in this line (it does not, however, tell us if we're going to marry. That's the marriage and children line). Normally, the Heart Line begins on the outside of the palm beneath the pinky (above the Head Line) and ends below the index finger. If it ends between the index and middle fingers, this indicates a realistic approach to relationships— unless it goes all the way up to the fingers' creases, which suggests serious, overly idealistic expectations. A Heart Line that stops beneath the middle finger is indicative of a somewhat selfish nature in matters of the heart. If it dips down toward the thumb, the person may have a deep-seated need for attention. If there is only one line running across the palm, it's the Head Line. In this case, the head and heart lines

are
combined,
indicating that
the person's head
rules their heart. When these two lines run
together, reason and emotion are closely
entwined in the person's subconscious.

The longer and deeper the Heart Line, the warmer and deeper the affections. A short, thin line connotes a lack of emotional interests, but a short, deep line indicates stability in emotional dealings. A strong upward curve shows a romantic, loving nature. A relatively straight line indicates a somewhat dispassionate temperament, and a downward-dipping heart line means you're dealing with a cold fish. The closer the Heart Line runs to the base of the index finger, the happier and more stable the relationship. Smaller lines branching off the Heart Line denote multiple love affairs. Upward branches represent successful romances; downward branches indicate the opposite. A chained, broken, or wavery Heart Line indicates a fickle nature and many brief love interests. An island shows a period of depression, crosses or breaks indicate emotional loss, and chains represent emotional agitation. A star anywhere on the line is a sign of marital bliss. A fork at the end of this line could mean the person has their choice of romantic partners. An extra (sister) Heart Line strengthens the qualities of this line. People with this double line have great emotional strength (although it can also represent a longing for an emotionally supportive partner).

THE SECONDARY LINES

If the primary lines show our approach to the world, then the secondary lines (fate, fame, health) show the world's effect on us. These three lines offer more in the way of commentary, and serve to embellish the information found in the primary lines. It is not uncommon for some of these lines to be completely absent from a person's palm.

The Fate (or Destiny) Line doesn't represent a person's destiny as much as it does ambitions and progress in life. It shows the impact of society and world events on the person's life. It traditionally begins in the middle of the palm near the wrist and runs straight up toward the middle finger. A line that begins very low on the hand is the sign of someone who had early ambitions. A line that starts farther up in the hand suggests a decision made later in life. A long, solid line is the sign of a confident, decisive person. In many cases, the line runs up the hand in fits and starts.

A Fate Line that arises in the Life Line indicates a self-willed individual who found success by taking destiny into his or her own hands. If it starts separately but then runs with the Life Line, this indicates that the person had to put self-interest aside to appease other people. The point at which it begins to run on its own again is the point at which the individual began living for the self again. A Fate Line that stops at the head line suggests that the person had a goal and achieved it; if it picks up again later, it indicates that a new goal has been undertaken (this configuration could also mean that the person changed careers or lifestyles, and found fulfillment in doing so). If the Fate Line stops at the Heart Line, a romantic relationship may hinder the person's career. If the Fate Line is small—or absent altogether—it doesn't mean the person lacks ambition; it simply means this person is independent and achieves goals on his or her own terms. Smaller lines branching off the Fate Line suggest that the person's destiny is influenced by the primary line to which they point. Islands or breaks in the Fate Line indicate setbacks, periods of hard luck, or disruptions in one's progress. A star at the end of the Fate Line is the mark of success. Squares represent protection from danger; small lines crossing the Fate Line show times when other people oppose the person's desires. A doubled Fate Line doubles good fortune.

The Fame Line pertains to the role of public recognition in the subject's life and reinforces the Fate Line (they run parallel to each other). The longer the line, the more likely it is that the person will be well known. Those who lack this line may be successful, but they won't experience public acclaim. It usually begins on the heel of the hand (in the Mount of the Moon) and runs up toward the ring finger. If the Fame Line arises in the Fate Line, it means that the person will find a fulfilling, successful career. A line that starts low on the hand suggests early popularity; if it begins farther up the hand, it indicates that success comes late in the person's life. If this line is faint, short, or absent, it means the person is one who'll have to struggle to achieve recognition. If the line runs especially close to the ring finger, it indicates fame through artistic pursuits; if it's also capped by a star, it shows spectacular success. A square on the Fame Line represents a kindly patron, and a doubled Fame Line increases public awareness. As

with the Fate Line, any
smaller lines
branching
off this

Fate

Health Fame

line
must be
evaluated in terms of
the major lines to which they
point. An island indicates a deeply-felt disap-

pointment. A broken line indicates the ups and downs of public popularity.

The Health Line is considered an annotation to the conditions shown by the Life Line, although it also comments on material wealth. The Health Line begins under the little finger, and runs diagonally down the hand toward the base of the thumb. The longer the line, the more robust the health of the individual. A very short line is a sign of medical problems, but the absence of this line signals good health. If the person is missing the Fate and Fame Lines, this line helps in evaluating their success in making money . A strong, straight line is indicative of business savvy as well as the energy needed to work hard and make money. A wavery line connotes a frail constitution. Breaks, islands, or crosses on this line indicate times when health needs to be carefully monitored. Breaks or chains represent business problems caused by poor health, and an island indicates possible hospitalization. A square on the Health Line represents beneficent, protective forces at work.

THE MINOR LINES AND SPECIAL MARKINGS

The minor lines show special attributes and events in life and, with the special markings, reveal the life experience.

The Girdle of Venus is a semicircular line that begins between the index and middle fingers and runs across the upper middle palm to the spot between the ring finger and pinky. This line supplements the information found in the Heart Line. The presence of the Girdle has erotic implications; it indicates a strong interest in sex and a very sensual nature. It is also the sign of a sensitive, highly emotional person. If the Girdle is distinct, the sex drive is unusually active, and the person may waste too much time and energy in pursuit of carnal pleasures. If the Girdle is broken and runs in fits and starts, it indicates that the person tends to have many sexual encounters but can't find emotional fulfillment in a relationship. If this line is missing, it suggests that the person's emotions are controlled.

The Lines of Marriage and Children are indicated by small, slash-like marks that begin on the outside of the hand just below the pinky and run toward the ring finger. When evaluating this line, also consider the properties of the Heart Line and Girdle of Venus. Usually, there will be several light, feathery lines representing brief romantic encounters, and one or more deeper, more distinct lines that represent actual marriages. One long, clear line denotes a strong, happy union that will last a lifetime. Little lines that run up from the top of this line (but don't intersect it) indicate the number of children that will be born into that relationship. If the marriage line runs all the way to the ring finger it indicates that there's a tremendous—almost spiritual—connection between the partners; these relationships can be extremely happy. If there is more than one marriage line, the lower line represents the first marriage; the upper lines, a second, third, and so on. If there is only one Marriage Line, the closer to the base of the pinky it is, the later in life the union will be. If there is one distinct Marriage Line next to a thinner line, it means that in addition to their main relationship, the person has another very intimate relationship, which can be emotional or physical in nature. Vertical lines crossing through the Marriage Line indicate an argumentative relationship. If all the lines are light, it suggests a number of relationships but no marriages. But it's important to note that these lines aren't always accurate, because we do have the free will to make our own decisions in life. So if, for example, there are two Marriage Lines, this doesn't guarantee that the person will be wed twice, it just suggests that such a thing is *possible*. A fork at the beginning of a Marriage Line indicates a long engagement or that a relationship was begun for the wrong reasons. A fork at the end suggests that the partners have very different opinions; it may also indicate a separation (but not necessarily of a permanent nature). A line that breaks and then starts again by overlapping indicates a separation followed by a reunion. An island in the line represents a period of trouble; if the line continues, the problems were resolved. A line crossing the end of the Marriage Line (to form a capital T) means that the relationship is over.

The Ring of Solomon circles the index finger; it begins between the middle and forefingers and runs to the outside of the palm under the index finger. This line suggests an innate capacity for intellectual reasoning, and comments favorably on the person's intuitive, empathetic nature and spiritual potential. A broken or fragmented line is the sign of a good listener. If the line runs deep into the Mount of Jupiter, it means the person is selfless and altruistic. The absence of this line suggests a very rational approach to thoughts and behavior.

The Ring of Saturn circles the middle finger; it starts between the middle and index fingers and ends between the middle and ring fingers. If the line is solid, it means the person tends to brood. An uneven line indicates despair and possibly suicidal tendencies.

Fortunately, the Ring of Saturn is rarely seen. Although this line mirrors the Girdle of Venus, the latter is more widely spaced.

The Line of Mars originates on the inside of the hand above the thumb and mirrors the Life Line. This line represents the person's approach toward adversity and the strength of the life force. The longer the line, the more firm the individual's resolve. A short line indicates bravery. If this line is absent, it's indicative of a dependent nature.

Travel Lines start on the edge of the palm on the heel of the hand and fan up and out. The length and strength of the lines show the distance travelled and the importance of the trip. One distinct line suggests a permanent move to a distant location. Usually, the Travel Lines indicate major journeys (cross-country, overseas) that have a profound effect on the person. Many light lines can indicate a jet-set lifestyle, with lots of travel but nothing of particular significance. When a Travel Lines intersects the Life Line, it means that a trip will be made for health reasons, or that the person's health will be affected by the journey.

The Money Line runs from the base of the thumb to below the other fingers. It indicates a person who has innate money-making abilities. A line that ends beneath the index finger and is capped by a star is the sign of someone who attracts money like a magnet. Wealth that comes through an inheritance is indicated by a line that stops under the pinky. Money made in business is represented by a line that runs to the middle finger. Money that comes as a lucky surprise is indicated by a line that runs from the Head Line to below the ring finger and intersects the Fame Line.

The Thumb Chain circles the base of the thumb; it is a sign of obstinacy.

The Bracelets are lines that circle the wrist and base of the palm. They offer additional insight into the other lines. They are generally considered signs of good fortune, unless the top line points up toward the middle of the hand, which is a health warning. Clear, distinct bracelets represent positive conditions. If the bracelets are broken or frayed, it means there will be obstacles on the path of life. If a bracelet swings up into the palm to connect with the Fate Line, it may signal a future inheritance. Any smaller lines branching off the bracelets into the palm should be taken as important references to the major lines toward which they point.

Lines of Opposition arise on the outside of the palm, between the head and heart lines, and run across the hand between the two. They show opposition or setbacks that one must deal with in the course of life. This line is often accompanied by a Battle Cross in the center of the palm.

The Line of Intuition is a semicircular line that begins on the heel of the hand and swings up through the palm to the area between the head and heart lines. This line is a link between the physical impulses from the outside world and the intellectual qualities of the inner self. It is found in people with a very keen sense of intuition.

The Line of Escape begins on the base of the thumb and fans out into the palm. It is usually found on someone who can't readily cope with the difficulties of life. If the line runs into the Fate Line, it suggests that the person escapes into their imagination or the creative arts. If it intersects the Health Line, it could mean that the person uses drugs or alcohol as a means of escape.

Some hands are relatively clear and smooth, with only the primary lines clearly marked, while others are a patchwork of tiny lines and special markings that are significant in themselves. Clear, smooth hands indicate a clear, smooth life with few problems. Lines fretting the palm show many events and lots of nervous tension. Sometimes the special markings are closely connected with the lines or mounts. Such markings show events connected with the area of life that the particular line or mount governs. Other markings are more free-floating, and their meaning depends on where they appear. In general, small vertical lines represent talent and potential, while horizontal lines indicate fruitless efforts. Chains denote disturbances or tension; and islands or circles show difficult periods (although a circle on the Mount of Apollo indicates great success). Triangles are also a sign of success and good fortune; squares symbolize protection and security; crosses denote opposition; stars signal sudden change or surprising lucky events (except on the life line). Dots and bars represent obstacles. Breaks indicate a change of direction, and forks at the end of a line show dispersion or deterioration. The appearance of a grid (tiny crosshatched lines) indicates opposition; a series of small lines—vertical or horizontal—represent unusual grit and determination.

There are also two special crosses that appear on the palm: The Battle Cross, which appears in the triangle formed by the life, head and health lines, marks people who are willing to make sacrifices for a cause. It also connotes a tendency toward reckless living or a quarrelsome nature. The Mystic Cross lies in the middle of the palm between the head and heart lines. It denotes a person who will sacrifice material possessions for spiritual enlightenment.